But Does it Scan?
by
Colin McAlister

To Jim, on the occasion of our Bard's 250th anniversary.

Best wishes & I hope you enjoy it

January 2009

But Does it Scan?

Colin McAllister

ATHENA PRESS
LONDON

BUT DOES IT SCAN?
Copyright © Colin McAllister 2008

All Rights Reserved

No part of this book may be reproduced in any form
by photocopying or by any electronic or mechanical means,
including information storage or retrieval systems,
without permission in writing from both the copyright
owner and the publisher of this book.

ISBN: 978 1 84748 426 0

First published 2008 by
ATHENA PRESS
Queen's House, 2 Holly Road
Twickenham TW1 4EG
United Kingdom

Printed for Athena Press

To Agnes Milne, without whose encouragement this book would never have been published.

Author's Note

Most of these poems are one-tenth inspiration and nine-tenths perspiration. Some appeared out of nowhere and almost wrote themselves. Enjoy them for what they are – mostly just pieces of fun.

Contents

Latin America

Latin American Odyssey	13
Latin American Odyssey Part Two	18
Latin American Odyssey Part Three	21
Through Peru	23

Computing

To a Mouse	27
To a Computer	29
Computer Problems	31
Know the Basics	32

St Andrews

The Wheelie Bin	37
The Red Tar	38
An Appeal to the Youth of St Andrews	39
St Andrews	40

St Andrews Golf

The Dunhill Cup at St Andrews, 1988	45
A Tale	46
The Bonnie Links o' St Aundraes	47
Sweet Swilcan	48
The Red Flag	50
Whins, Will We See Your Like Again?	51
To Another Mouse	52
Bonnie Green Thing	53
Ae Long Swing	54

Miscellaneous

To Maggie, On Slipping her Disc	59
Sonnet: Foot and Mouth Disease	60
The Tayside Police	61
The Caledonian Canal	62
On a Virgin Atlantic Flight from Gatwick to Orlando	63
Donald and Sue Coid	64
Malcolm Mitchell and Frances Foster	66
Professor Edward Belt	68

American Politics

The Donkey and the Elephant – A Fable	71
Presidential Election Limericks	72
2004 Election Limericks	74
Further 2004 Election Limericks	76
US Presidential Election 2008	77

Religious

Sonnet: A Prayer for a Happy Life and a Happy Death	81
What Really Matters	82
Sonnet: The Love of Jesus	83
Sonnet: Life and Death	84
Sonnet: Life's Journey	85
Easter Thoughts	86

Glossary 87

Latin America

Latin American Odyssey

In the autumn of 2005
I ventured from my Scottish hive
On a Latin American cruise,
Replete with good food and lots of booze.

It was from Belize that we set sail;
With luck we missed both hurricane and gale.
At Placencia beach we first landed,
Having been in Zodiacs all banded.

From Puerto Cortez we look a bus
To Copan ruins – it was worth the fuss.
We learned how to read the Mayan glyphs
And how a king was killed in tribal tiffs.

To Utila Island next we sailed,
Where snorkellers and birdwatchers both prevailed.
To Coxen Hole on island Roatan
Along the Honduras coast next we ran.

Other islands off the Mosquito Coast
We saw – but that is all that I can boast.
Big Corn and Little Corn Islands, alas,
Had seas too rough for Zodiacs to pass.

Bocas del Toro in Panama
Is not the place for a Pa and Ma,
For there you'll find the Nasty Mermaid bar,
A haunt for drinkers from near and far.

Popa Island is girdled with mangroves,
It has not much room for sandy coves,
But there is at least one sandy reach –
It goes by the name of Red Frog Beach.

At last we reached the Panama Canal –
It does not disappoint, it's not banal.
We saw lots of birds and a crocodile –
I thought they only swam in the Nile!

I speak not as a contrarian –
Next we landed on the coast of Darien,
Where we saw the Embera Indians dance.
Those ladies had us all in a trance!

The next day at sea, we crossed the line
Where King Neptune extorted his fine.
On All Saints Day we arrived at Ecuador,
Preceded by many a Conquistador.

At Agua Blanca we took a walk,
Enlivened by lots of avian talk,
But the fishing town of Puerto Lopez
Was not adorned by even one des res.

About the Isla de la Plata
I cannot talk – there's just too much data.
But flying gracefully around the shore,
Blue-footed boobies you'll see by the score.

Next we came ashore at Trujillo,
Where our lunch was a *bocadillo*.
Those citadels built of adobe
Looked like something from the desert Gobi.

And so at length we came to Callao.
It's the port of Lima, you must allow.
And there for some the journey will end
As they bid farewell to many a new friend.

I have this to say about the staff,
They've given us many a good laugh!
Who is the rapier-witted cartoonist,
Who rises in the morning the soonest?

There is Hannah, She who must be obeyed;
Alwyn, who tells when the table is laid;
Krista, too, who works behind the bar –
She has travelled and will travel far.

Carol gave a talk on the iguana,
Gary on the land that's called Gondwana,
John has lectured on the birds called frigates
And also on buccaneers and pirates.

Dennis told us of the types of banana
Found in the Caribbean panorama.
Patty taught all about the world's mangroves
And superstitions of salty old coves.

We've heard about the Mayan Calendar
And how it is superior by far,
Because the Earth's orbit is elliptic,
And why the Egyptians speak in Coptic.

Of passengers there were forty-three,
That's forty-two of you and one of me.
Some of them came from the United States,
Some of them from Canada – all shipmates.

Two of them were from Lithuania
Gripped by the selfsame travel mania.
There was a lady from Northumbria,
In Italy she'd been, down in Umbria.

There was also Hubert, that old sea dog,
He knew well how to write a Captain's log,
And Joan, the lady from Syracuse, NY,
Who always wanted to know the reason why.

There were eight Aussies, from Port Macquarie,
When we say 'Goodbye', I'll be most sorry.
To Doug and Lois, and the rest of that crew
I'll say 'G'day, the best of luck to you.'

Of Doctor Bill and his wife, Hilary
I'll not say anything in pillory.
In Nova Scotia live Bob and Penny –
No more jokes for you – I've told too many.

If there are some that I have left out
It is because I've not words with you to clout.
I hope by this I've not you offended.
Besides, the least said, the soonest mended.

I hope these lines written in leisure
Have given you something of pleasure,
And as we go our different ways
I hope you'll think, 'Those were happy days.'

Latin American Odyssey
Part Two

The Pelican

Have you seen a pelican crossing
The Equator with waves a-tossing?
It is a sight, I you assure,
That in your mind will long endure.
Not much can be more engrossing!

The Booby

The booby of Peru and Chile
Is really but a silly billy.
From Peru to Positano,
It deposits its white guano
Onto the heads of tourists, willy-nilly.

The Dolphin

Joyful dolphins, without trammel,
Are not classed as fish, but mammal.
Friendly they are, as friendly can be,
Disporting playfully in the sea.
Do you know a nicer animal?

The Inca Tern

The quite beautiful Inca tern
Is very easy to discern,
Sitting on the ship's lines at Callao
Or perched forward on the ship's prow,
Hoping thereby a fish to earn.

The Albatross

Over all the sea birds, the albatross
Reigns supreme – it is the boss.
Gliding gracefully over the sea,
It's a delight to you and me.
Who would kill it? I'm at a loss.

The Lizard

The Patagonian lizard
Is known for its gorgeous gizzard.
If an Andean albatross
Ever happens its path to cross,
It goes and hides itself in a blizzard.

The Whale

The kings of the oceans are the whales –
They are not bothered by the gales.
Whether killer, sperm, fin or sei,
They dive deeply in search of their prey,
While giving a flourish with their tails.

The Rhea

The rhea's cousin to the emu,
Although a bird of different hue,
And even if you think it quite rich,
Another cousin is the ostrich.
This zoology is known to few!

The Zorro

I must confess, to my sorrow,
I did not know there was a zorro!
In the Torres del Paine Park,
I hope to see one before dark –
If not today, then tomorrow.

The Guanaco

The guanaco is sib to the llama,
But you'll find none in the Atacama –
It prefers the southern Andes,
Where it ranks among the dandies,
Supreme in its mountain panorama.

The Penguin

The small Magellanic penguin
Can't be bettered as a friend in
The Weddell Sea or Sea of Ross
(Home to many an albatross),
Seas with no start and with no ending.

Latin American Odyssey Part Three

The Pilots

Dagoberto and Marcelo,
Two Chileans with a cello,
Came on our ship at Puerto Montt,
To guide *Polar Star* as was their wont,
So let's greet them with a big 'Hello'!

Cinco Hermanos

At Cinco Hermanos at a whim,
The bravest of us had a swim.
From ice-cold to near-boiling spring,
The colour to our cheeks it did bring,
Bathing at the Pacific Rim.

Torres del Paine

About Park Torres del Paine,
Gary gave a talk most brainy.
There are lumps of granite called plutons,
And other rocks known as moutons.
What a shame the day was rainy.

The Beagle Channel

Sailing through the channel Beagle,
You don't need the eyes of an eagle
To see the wildlife all around,
Truly the place does with it abound,
Petrel, Arctic tern or Dolphin gull.

Cape Horn

We had a Norwegian called Jorn,
Whose aspect was somewhat forlorn.
He took us ashore by Zodiac,
Driving it as would a maniac,
Until at last we rounded Cape Horn.

Ushuaia

This trip started with the Maya,
Along the way we've eaten papaya.
We've sailed in the Caribbean
And seen the mountains Andean,
Now my last word is Ushuaia!

Through Peru

Our courier Anne is a Yorkshire lass,
A guide whom I'm sure none can surpass.
It seems that no one else will do the trick,
So here are some words – but I'll make it quick.

We have suffered from altitude sickness
And have seen Inca walls of great thickness,
We've learned that coca tea cures all known ills –
It's better even than those Beecham pills.

Our local guides Alec and Freddy
Were always there, willing and ready.
They told us how the Incas were slain
And their gold taken to the land of Spain.

If you drink one too many Pisco Sour,
Your head will feel like Pisa's Leaning Tower.
I confess 'El Condor Pasa's' refrain
Is now fairly embedded in my brain.

In Peru we've seen Lake Titicaca
And, here and there, many an alpaca.
I thought floating islands were a dessert –
That they are made of reeds, I now assert.

Twelve days we've been here in Peru
And this is our last night, which we all rue.
So, before the parting of the ways,
We thank you, Anne, for these happy days.

Computing

To a Mouse

Wee sleekit, electronic beastie,
O what a current's in thy breastie!
Thou need na click awa sae hasty,
On speedy screen!
I wad be laith to unplug thee
From thy demesne!

I'm truly sorry the computer's speed
Has the human brain quite left for deid,
An' justifies that ill opinion
Which makes men grumble
At thee, thou electronic marvel,
Be thou e'er sae humble!

I doubt na, whyles, but thou may blink;
What then? Weel then, here's what I think!
Ilka body has a virus –
It's no uncommon; are na computers just like us,
An' almaist human!

Thy wee bit program's got a bug,
Thy silver screen's the breakfast o' a dug!
An' naething I ken o' what to do,
It's got me beat! An' soon the hale world will ca' me mug.
An' fule complete!

Thou kens thy spreadsheets through and through,
An' what wi' Windows thou canst do,
An' sae thou thocht, thou hadst it made,
But it wasna long
Before thy passwords were gainsaid
An' proved thee wrong.

That program that was so well written,
Now wi' a bug is badly bitten,
An' the computer's worse than useless,
Nor any guid.
By a human hand, thou's been smitten,
Nor by a squid.

But, Mousie, thou art no thy lane
In proving computing may be in vain:
The best programs o' mice an' men
Gang aft agley
An' lea'e us nought but grief an' pain
For promised joy!

Still thou art blest, compared wi' me!
The off switch gies guid rest to thee;
But thou giest bad dreams tae me,
O' technofear! My job next year I canna see,
My prospect's drear!

To a Computer

Fair fa' your electronic face,
Great chieftain o' the TV race!
Abune them a' ye tak your place,
PC's your name;
Weel are ye wordy of a place
Within my hame.

The corner of my room ye fill,
You're ready aye to serve my will,
Your memory I can access still
In time o' need,
While on your screen the pixels spill
For me to read.

Then see your face licht up sae bricht,
Wi' your eldritch flickerin' licht,
Working tirelessly through the nicht,
Like onie witch;
And then, gieing the answers richt,
Without a hitch!

Then computer buffs stretch and strive,
This their boast: the best hard-disk drive,
Till a' their weel-swall'd bytes belyve
Can do their sums;
Then Computerman, maist like a hive,
'Bethankit' hums.

Is there that owre his pen and ink,
That had the time an ee tae blink,
Or ever that had dared to think
How great's your speed?
It's faster than a curling rink –
He's left for deid!

Poor devil! See him owre his task,
Unequal to what his job may ask,
He's got nae time like sharks to bask
Or even think;
Weaker than beer made outwith a cask,
Unfit to drink!

But mark the geek, computer-mad,
For him his work is no sae bad,
Clap in his haund a mouse, he's glad.
For hours he'll sit;
He'll even buy his mouse a pad,
Nor work will quit.

Bill Gates, wha's dollars and to spare,
A' made through your computing flair,
Oor Scotland wants nae auld software –
Parritch and claes!
But, if you wish her grateful prayer,
Gie her Windaes!

Computer Problems

If you have got a computer problem,
Then I to you will divulge my system:
If ever your computer goes down,
My advice is not to scowl at it or frown,
But to smile instead benignly and think,
Whatever could have made it go on the blink?
Try out each cause; whatever remains –
That is the cause of your computer's pains.
A cause unusual is the ghost modem –
This is when two are running in tandem –
The computer doesn't know which to choose,
Which, for the user, is very bad news.

Know the Basics

About computers I was in the dark.
Before I joined the class of Wendy Clark.
Truly, I was an IT dinosaur,
Computers I feared like the Minotaur.

I knew not that computers had towers
And to use them was beyond my powers.
Yet I had heard about the floppy disk,
But to use one seemed far too great a risk.

Now that I've learned a mouse to click,
I no longer feel that I'm very thick.
I used to think that I didn't have the nous,
But now a mouse is welcome in my house.

When upon the screen there comes an icon,
I no longer feel quite so woe begone.
And now I've learned the screen to scroll,
I really feel that I am on a roll.

Documents I've created and justified,
A process that used to leave me mystified.
With ease I minimise or maximise
And can adjust my text to any size.

Anything I can do, I can undo –
It's all there on the screen for me to view.
With toolbar and taskbar I've come so far
That, boasting apart, I am quite a star.

My documents now I'm able to save,
Hidden somewhere in the computer's cave.
I have no trouble in finding my files,
Now that I've mastered the computer's wiles.

I know now how to change the format –
I begin to think this is quite old hat –
And as for changing the styles or size of font,
I'd say this is a jolly sort of jaunt.

I do not mean to make a show of pride –
I can use the icon to show or hide
And I am now a better spellchecker,
Than the Chancellor of the Exchequer.

Now that I have finally learned the way to clipart,
I'm almost ready this course to depart.
The start was learning the mouse to point,
The finish will be using Powerpoint.

One thing I thought would have me well beat,
Was gaining mastery of the spreadsheet.
But even there I did not bend the knee,
The help of a good teacher was the key.

Wendy, I've enjoyed being in your class –
You really are a remarkable lass.
My time at Elmwood has not been all tint,
Providing I can get this thing to print!

St Andrews

The Wheelie Bin
Tune: O Tannenbaum

Oh, wheelie bin! Oh, wheelie bin!
What stinking rubbish lies within!
No matter that we're tired and old,
We'll wheel you out just as we're told.

Then push and pull out to the street,
Our garbage with its smell so sweet,
Though citizens their taxes pay,
The bureaucrats must have their way.

Beware Fife Council autocrats
And all Glenrothes bureaucrats;
The greatest of your many sins
Is introducing wheelie bins.

Oh, wheelie bin! Oh, wheelie bin!
Your masters needna think they'll win!
We Fifers arena servile men –
Tell the Council tae think again!

The Red Tar

The people's tar is deepest red,
It covers now the roadway bed.
No matter that our streets are wrecked,
It is politically correct!

Then spread the red tar far and wide,
So bicyclists can have their ride.
Though citizens express their views,
We will their council tax abuse.

Democracy is but a sham,
Down people's throats our views we'll ram.
The people's potholes we will not fill,
Instead we'll make them do our will!

An Appeal to the Youth of St Andrews

I'd like to speak to those of younger hide,
Why in our town take you so little pride?
Perhaps I'm speaking to the deaf and dumb –
Why mess up our streets with your chewing gum?

Do not think that I am old and bitter,
But please will you avoid dropping your litter?
We all live in a town of such great charm,
We should avoid doing it any harm.

From what I write, it will be evident
That I am a St Andrews resident.
One day you will be old and then will blame
The youngsters of St Andrews just the same.

So, youngsters buck up and mend your ways
And help keep St Andrews a town to praise.

*Vicus Australis Incola**

---

* South Street inhabitant

St Andrews

What is it I love about St Andrews?
Is it the history or the great views?
What is it about this piece of space,
That makes me want its grey stones to embrace?

Muckross, the promontory of the boar,
Was its first name, in Pictish days of yore;
Then Kilrymont, the church on the royal hill,
A name that in the town is remembered still.

Bishop Acca, you brought St Andrew's bones,
And are now interred under Hexham's stones!
Bishop Robert, you built our cathedral grand
That for centuries in splendour did stand!

Along St Andrews streets in days gone by,
Hordes of pilgrims would catch the eye.
They came to honour one of the Lord's friends,
Singing his praises going through the Pends.

The university – it's Scotland's first –
Was founded to slake Scottish scholars' thirst.
Bishop Kennedy and Benedict XIIIth
Made St Andrews in Europe the fourteenth.

The Morrises, golfers of great renown,
What prestige you have given to our town!
Allan Robertson, Tom Kidd – our town's sons –
Were also great golfing champions.

This place of golf, church, university,
This special place beside the North Sea,
Can sometimes be a claustrophobic trap,
But there's no better place upon the map.

St Andrews Golf

The Dunhill Cup at St Andrews, 1988

Tune: The Ball of Kirriemuir

Four and twenty golfers came down to St Andrews.
When the week was over, one had made the news.
Singing Faldo hit it this time, Faldo hit it noo,
He wouldnae hit it last time, he didnae hae a view.

Greg Norman, he was there, trying for a record score;
But then at the Road Hole he could only get a four.
Rodger Davis, he was there, having a splendid round;
He came to the Road Hole and sliced it out of bounds.

Curtis Strange, he was there, looking very pleased,
Until he missed a putt – he said a lady sneezed.
Seve Ballesteros, he was there, well below his best –
'The way I'm playing,' he said, 'I surely need a rest.'

Mark James, he was there, in the English side,
He said, 'These Scots, they cannot us abide.'
The Canadian team, they were there, flying the Maple Leaf,
But the Shamrocks beat them and put them all to grief.

The Welsh team, they were there, giving it a try,
Until the Road Hole bunker put some sand into their eye.
Eamonn D'Arcy, he was there, leading the Irish team,
They won so much money – it was better than a dream.

A Tale

One evening by the R&A
I saw a sight that was full fey.
Atop a chairback I saw a skull –
The firelight showed it somewhat dull –
And then I heard a donkey bray
Or perhaps it was a horse's neigh.
From that chair it came – a mighty roar.
Oh, heavens, how that skull did snore!
I looked again – some trick of light –
It was no skull, it was Jimmy White.
Outside, the moonbeams were so bright,
The R&A was a shining white.
Then to the skull I shouted 'Fore!'
And out it sallied through the door
And then, oh what a hideous sight,
Empty sockets froze me with fright,
Chattering teeth that had lost their bite,
Once quite clean, but now off-white!
To the Swilken Brig I took my flight,
The ghouls darena cross its ancient height!
Safe at home, having crossed the Brig,
Of Cutty Sark I took a swig.
I slept that night, but in the morning
I thocht it might hae been a warning –
Drinking too much when you are drouthy
Can make you see things maist uncouthy.
So if you take a dram tonight,
Remember the skull of Jimmy White.

The Bonnie Links o' St Aundraes
Tune: The Bonnie Banks of Loch Lomond

By yon bonnie links where I aince used to play,
Where the sun shines bright on St Aundraes,
Where me and my golf ball were ever wont to stray
On the bonnie, bonnie links o' St Aundraes.

O you'll hit a high drive and I'll hit a low drive
And I'll be on the green afore you –
But me and my golf ball will never meet again
On the bonnie, bonnie links o' St Aundraes.

It was there that we parted in yon prickly whin,
On the right-hand side o' the seventh,
Where in purple hue the Angus hills we view
And the fairway crosses the eleventh.

A wee birdie putt and my step has a spring
And in sunshine the fairways are basking,
But a foozled drive it gets nae second chance again,
Though your partners their laughter are masking.

Sweet Swilcan

Tune: 'Sweet Afton' by Robert Burns

Flow gently, sweet Swilcan, among thy fairways!
Flow gently, I'll sing thee a song in thy praise!
My golf ball is sunk in thy murmuring stream –
Flow gently, sweet Swilcan, in silence I'll scream!

Thou seagull, whose screech resounds through the course,
Ye wild whistling blackbirds in yon thorny gorse,
Thou high-hovering lark, thy trilling forbear.
I charge you, disturb not my swing onie mair.

How testing, sweet Swilcan, thy neighbouring links,
All covered with golfers since daylight's first blinks.
There daily I wander, as noon rises high,
The flight of my golf ball I follow by eye.

How pleasant the holes and greens nearby where you flow,
Where wild on the golf course the gorse bushes grow.
There oft as mild evening sweeps over the sea
The sweet-scented gorse bush hides my golf ball from me.

Thy crystal stream, Swilcan, how lovely it glides
And winds by the green where my golf ball oft bides.
How often my golf ball thy water does claim,
As glowering at my golf club it challenges my game!

Flow gently, sweet Swilcan, among thy fairways!
Flow gently, sweet river, the theme of my lays!
My golf ball is sunk in thy murmuring stream –
Flow gently, sweet Swilcan, in silence I'll scream!

The Red Flag
Tune: 'O Tannenbaum'

On the links, greenkeepers were deployed,
The Road Hole bunker they have destroyed.
No matter what local golfers say,
St Andrews Links Trust must have its way!

Then raise the protest far and wide,
Let locals' views not be denied!
As golfers shudder at the news,
The Links Trust does its place abuse.

One thing alone will purge their shame
And safeguard the Road Hole's good name:
The Road Hole bunker they must restore
And leave alone for evermore.

Whins, Will We See Your Like Again?

Tune: O Tannenbaum

O Old Course whins, O Old Course whins!
To cut you down would be a sin.
You have been there since days of old,
Yet your bell the Links Trust has tolled!

O Old Course gorse, O Old Course gorse!
For years you've beautified our course.
Yet the Links Trust has cut you down.
Old Tom Morris, how he would frown!

Woe to you, St Andrews Links Trust!
Trim our gorse bushes if you must;
But our golf courses you have vandalised.
If the world knew, they'd be scandalised!

O Old Course whin, O Old Course whin!
I hope that soon you'll grow again.
The Old Lady just now is stripped.
Those who ordered this should be sheep-dipped!

To Another Mouse

Wee sneaky opportunist beastie,
Wha has my Mars bar in thy breastie!
Thou'd better start awa' fu' hasty,
Wi bickering brattle!
I amna laith to run an chase thee,
An' gie thee battle!

I ken that thou maun be a thief,
But what thou did beggars a' belief!
A hole thou's gnawed in my gowf bag,
To get my sweet.
I'll needs buy anither to drag
Wi weary feet!

But Mousie, I'll forgive thee yet,
For thy living thou has to get.
Mars bars thou had better forget
An' eat nae mair!
For if thou eat ma gowfing fare,
I'll mak thee sair!

Mice can bring out the best o' me.
A man that can forgive, you see,
Will be the best a man can be,
You can depend!
But when hatred blends a man's ee,
He's no true friend!

Bonnie Green Thing

Tune: Bonnie Wee Thing by Robert Burns

Bonnie green thing, cannie green thing,
Old Course green wi' grass sae fine!
In summer I'll cut and roll thee
And in winter thee will tine.

Truthfully I'm full o' anguish
As I see that grass o' thine,
Trampit doon wi' golfers doltish,
Wi' handicaps o' more than mine!

Rain and sun they make thy measure
And thy speed determines the line.
To putt on thee is pure pleasure
Greens o' Old Course sae divine!

Ae Long Swing

Tune: Ae Fond Kiss by Robert Burns

Ae long swing, my best endeavour!
Follow through – it flies for ever!
Deep in prickly whins I'll lodge thee,
Onto holding greens I'll wedge thee.
Who shall say that golf it grieves him,
While the star of hope it leaves him?
Me, nae cheerful twinkle lights me,
Dark despair around benights me,

I'll ne'er blame my wooden putter,
Nae swearwords my mouth will utter!
But to play golf is to love it
Love but it, and love for ever.
Had I never golfed sae madly,
Had I never golfed sae badly,
Never tried – or never started –
I had ne'er been broken-hearted.

Nae mair will I tak my driver,
Never chance mair than a fiver,
But noo ma golfing's just for fun
And I shake hands when a' is done.
Had I never swung sae quickly,
I'd not found the whins sae prickly,
Never lost – nor penalised –
My golf dream I'd hae realised.

Fare-you-weel, you Old Course fairways!
You to me were Heaven's stairways!
Yours be ilka joy and treasure,
Peace, enjoyment, love and pleasure!
Ae long swing, my best endeavour!
Follow through – it flies for ever!
Down the middle straight I'll send thee,
Onto holding greens I'll wend thee.

Miscellaneous

To Maggie, on Slipping her Disc

The number of times you've slipped your disc – it
Breaks all records and takes the dog's biscuit!
Next, no doubt, you'll write, 'My neck, I've cricked it,
Please, dear Colin, could you come and fix it?'

Now the purpose of this little refrain
Is to comfort you on your bed of pain;
The moral of your sorry tale is plain –
From cooking for bachelors you should abstain.

And, to conserve your sacroiliac,
Serve 'em up instead an aphrodisiac.
(If it is menus for this that you lack,
This one'll turn a man into a maniac –

Some pints of Guinness with oysters will do,
Or perhaps a mussel-and-onion stew,
But Batchelor's soup is a dreadful brew;
Give them instead Maggi's – it's worthy of you!)

Sonnet: Foot and Mouth Disease

The source of the outbreak of foot and mouth
Is found not in the North, but in the South.
The cause of this disease most sinister
Lies within the Palace of Westminster.

Over the years, the government's cut in half
Monies that they provided to the MAFF*,
Which left the nation's vets upon their knees
And unable to cope with the disease.

The EU also bears part of the blame,
Changing as they did the rules of the game –
Stock once went to their local abbatoir,
Now the EU further travel does require.

Blame not animals with a cloven hoof –
It's your politician that is the real coof!

---

* MAFF: Ministry of Agriculture, Fisheries and Food

The Tayside Police

The cameras of the Tayside Police
Operate on the roads and do not cease
Unwary motorists to catch,
Who think they're driving at Brand's Hatch,
The Monte Carlo Rally or at Nice.

The penalties they lay on the line
Are three points and a £60 fine.
They will give your licence a scan
And you'll receive a six-month ban,
If your points already amount to nine.

The Caledonian Canal

The story I have to tell is banal –
It's of the Caledonian Canal –
(Thomas Telford the engineer's boast).
It runs from the North Sea to the West Coast,
Joining together all the Great Glen's lochs.
By a series of ingenious locks
(Of which the greatest is Neptune's Staircase),
Ships can easily climb from place to place.

On a Virgin Atlantic Flight from Gatwick to Orlando

Dear Richard Branson, Pauline McBride
Is someone in whom you can take much pride.
Her list of virtues is as long's my arm,
But chief of all is her Scottish charm.
Her passengers she tries hard to serve –
For this she does your award deserve.
Everything is done with a ready smile
And so with ease she did my heart beguile.

Hannah Beaton looks just like Jane Seymour,
The kind of woman men always dream for.
I met her for nine hours in the sky –
Such a shame to have to say goodbye.
Perhaps we'll meet on some other flight –
That for me would be a great delight.

I'll say this without need of urging –
It's better by far to fly with Virgin.
Beautiful girls you cannot surpass –
They made me feel I was really first class.

Donald and Sue Coid

There was a stunning Aussie girl called Sue,
Whose eyes were a cerulean blue.
In the outback, unemployed,
Her life was a bit of a void,
So she kept looking for something to do.

It was then she met a kangaroo,
Who was making a hullabaloo.
She said, 'My peace you've destroyed,
That noise will you please avoid –
A polite "how do you do" will do!'

The kangaroo said, 'G'day, mate, to you!
I'm afraid I must hop to the loo.
I'm sorry your peace I've destroyed.
It's my overactive thyroid
Which accounts for that hullabaloo!'

At this point there strolled into purview
An Englishman who knew what to do.
'My name is Doctor Donald Coid.
Just one thing you must avoid –
Guinness is no good for the likes of you!'

Then up spoke the Australian Sue,
'Good doctors in the outback are few –
Meeting you makes me overjoyed,
My spirits you've really buoyed.
Permit me some tea for you to brew.'

That is the story of Don and Sue
And how their friendship grew and grew;
In the outback of people devoid,
Their company they well enjoyed
And all thanks to a sick kangaroo.

So without any more to do,
I'll wish 'Happy Christmas' to you.
These lines I hope you've enjoyed,
Doctor Don and Mrs Sue Coid.
I hope a good New Year will ensue!

Malcolm Mitchell and Frances Foster

In the library working her roster
One day was the lovely Frances Foster,
When in came Malcolm to borrow a book
And decided to have another look.

Being expert in the marketing style,
He thought that quite soon her he would beguile;
But he erred about that Lancashire lass,
For she judged his patter was rather crass.

Talk of his golf did not her amuse,
But only served her to confuse;
Birdies, bogeys and eagles were the same,
What could be the point of this silly game?

Yet in Malcolm she did see some good,
Despite his endless talk of his three wood,
For between practising with his putter
Sometimes a word of sense he did utter.

After reading books in Aberystwyth,
Frances bought a home to live in Alyth,
But for Malcolm's sake she moved to Fife,
There to be his obedient wife.

If you think that a word of this is true,
Then no one is a bigger fool than you.
Fairy stories are for a children's book,
Which this is not, unless I am mistook.

The moral of this tale is plain:
Women to men can be blessing or bane.
Men to women can often be sublime,
But are women's fools most of the time.

Professor Edward Belt

Did you know that Professor Edward Belt
Claims his descent from a Scottish Celt?
Are we to take this with a pinch of salt
(For without proof it must go by default)?

He claims a forebear sought a fairyland
But ended up instead at Maryland.
This mishap put him into such deep dudgeon,
That he devised himself an escutcheon.

Claiming descent through a Mayor of York
(A man born before the time of the fork),
Is a threadbare tale that does unravel,
For in those days westbound few did travel.

So it strikes me that this tale has a fault
Which must speedily be brought to a halt.
A Mayor of York will not metamorphose
When as a fossil in chalk he does repose.

Finding the truth in genealogy
Is much the same as in geology.
Human ancestry is a palimpsest,
Layer piled on layer, all laid to rest.

American Politics

The Donkey and the Elephant – A Fable

In the American Republic of Chad,
A Presidential election they've just had.
After only some of the votes had been counted,
To near-equal numbers they had amounted.
This has left both the parties equally sad,
As both had coveted the Chad House for their pad.
All this was achieved without blood and Gore
(Those days are long gone and for evermore).
Then the news spread through the land like a Bush fire
That not all votes could be checked by the due date,
Which meant the donkey's hopes were now rather dire
And the elephant had the key to the gate,
Who then did trumpet, 'I'm this nation's new Sire!'
This tale's moral is: don't drag your chads in the mire,
If it is to the Chad House that you do aspire.

Presidential Election Limericks

1.

There was a VP called Gore,
Who was thought a bit of a bore.
'In the election we've had
We must count every chad –
That way I can level the score.'

2.

There was a Governor called Bush,
Whose Pop gave him considerable push.
'The chads we must not hand-count,
For to too many they might amount,
So let's call the count with a rush.'

3.

The story of George Bush versus Al Gore
Would send anyone off to sleep and snore.
Let's hope they can get it over
Or soon it will be Passover,
If they keep on counting for evermore.

4.

The rulings of the US Supreme Court
Are more often long than they are short;
But in the Florida case,
They resolved to step up the pace
And decided the counting to abort.

5.

It's vote-counting time in Miami Dade
And this is how the game there is played:
Some votes they cheerfully will throw out,
Others get the benefit of the doubt
And the result depends upon how much you paid.

6.

We're all having fun in Tallahasee,
Cooking up some election fricassée.
The recipe is: add a chad or two to the rice,
To get a result that is rather nice
And murkier than the Zuyder Zee.

7.

This is tomorrow's weather Gorecast –
Very soon Al will breathe his last.
From Texas will come a Bush fire
That will stoke his funeral pyre
And that of every chad that's been cast.

2004 Election Limericks

1. Prologue

As the Presidential election day nears
And political partisans raise their cheers,
The result is in great doubt –
It depends on voter turnout –
But the winner will run the US for four years.

2. The Result

The election of 2004
Put President George Bush in charge once more.
The world was quite aghast
That his reign was not past,
As now more oil on the fires of war he will pour.

3. The Result that Wasn't

In 2004, George Bush was whacked
By John Kerry, whom the voters had backed.
Though the voting was near,
The result was quite clear –
President George Bush from the White House had been sacked.

On November 2nd 2004,
Senator Kerry wiped the electoral floor.
With an almighty push,
He ousted George W Bush
And sent him back to where he had come from before.

The election of 2004
To Senator Kerry opened the door.
The world heaved a sigh
And waved Bush bye-bye.
'Revenge is a dish best served cold,' said Al Gore.

4. Epilogue

By the election result I'm not impressed.
In fact, I am absolutely depressed.
The worst of my fears
Was four more Bush years.
How can that cowboy again be the leader of the West?

Further 2004 Election Limericks

George W Bush, the Texan pachyderm,
Is in the White House for a second term.
That so-smug political boll-weevil
Hears, sees and speaks but his axis of evil
And his re-election would make even a worm squirm.

The United States body politic
Knows every electoral dirty trick.
Now American people their votes have cast
And nailed their flag to the Republican mast –
A result sure to make every Democrat pig-sick!

US Presidential Election 2008

The US Presidential contest
Is quite an electoral slugfest.
But before the hopefuls enter the ring
Party caucuses their way must swing.

The process takes a huge amount of cash,
In search of which are made promises rash.
So, who do you think picks up the bill?
The winner doesn't, but the voters will.

I've forgotten most of the runners' names,
Their policies, and preposterous claims.
Two are left, Obama and John McCain.
But is the choice between them quite so plain?

The very young Senator Obama
Has support from a wide panorama.
Does he have enough political nous
If he were to make it to the White House?

John McCain may be considered too old,
But he has been a warrior bold.
So he's the man to support in the main,
When the chips are down, I'd go for McCain.

Religious

Sonnet: A Prayer for a Happy Life and a Happy Death

Lord, as I approach the end of my days,
May I love Thee in ever-better ways!
Take from me all human ambition,
Better then to seek Thy Volition.

Often I have wandered from Thy path –
Cleanse me now in Thy sacramental bath.
Support my steps on the final road
And lighten, I pray Thee, my sinful load.

Whatever trials I have yet to face,
Assist me to overcome by Thy grace.
Happily then shall I death await
As the opening of Thy heavenly gate.

Lord, may Thy love so my life inspire
That in Thy presence my soul may expire.

What Really Matters

If fortune your self-esteem flatters,
Or if life favours you in every way,
Or if the wheel should turn then, come what may,
You'll find that love is what really matters.

If your life lies in shreds and tatters,
Or if you lose your job or your wealth,
Or no longer are in the best of health,
You'll find then love is what really matters.

If life's rainstorm at your window batters,
Or mirth departs, leaving you only tears,
Or you're beset by advancing years,
You'll find then that love is what really matters.

If misfortune your family scatters,
Or former friendships fall far apart,
Or others' ingratitude chills your heart,
You'll find then that love is what really matters.

When by death your life's hourglass has been shattered,
And life has lost its passing pleasure,
You'll find this will be your lasting measure,
Love, was it for you what really mattered?

Sonnet: *The Love of Jesus*

The love of Jesus is all that matters –
Everything else is but rags and tatters.
Painful though it may be along the way,
Yet there is joy at the end of the day.

As I walk along life's weary road,
Often I want to unburden my load.
It's then that I hear a voice in the night –
'My yoke is easy and my burden light.'

Lord, You are 'the Way, the Truth and the Life'.
Grant me your help in life's battle and strife.
Often I lose heart and fall by the way,
Help me then to rise and continue the fray.

Lord, You know I am weak, but You are strong.
Help me to reach that home, for which I long.

Sonnet: Life and Death

O Lord, release me from my sins' deep mire
And burn in me but one great desire,
To love You better as each day goes by
And thus other sinners to You draw nigh.

Your love for me I cannot comprehend
And therefore my sins I cannot defend.
Your Grace overcomes all human weakness,
Nothing can withstand Your Divine Meekness.

Lord, You know that I am but made of clay,
Against You I sin almost every day.
Lord, despise not the work of Your Hands,
But help me live according to Your commands.

May I thus follow You along the Way,
To wake in death to the Light of Your Day.

Sonnet: Life's Journey

O Lord, how long before I see Your Face,
How long must I run in this earthly race?
As I enter into the final miles,
Help me to surmount life's steps and stiles.

You are my Hope and Your Love my Light,
Pointing the Way through the darkest night.
So by Faith may I reach the Promised Land
And my soul not be lost in Sinai's sand.

Often I stumble or lose the way,
Help and direct me by Thy Grace, I pray.
As I climb Thy celestial mountain,
Cleanse me in Thy sacramental fountain.

Then when I arrive, Lord, be it soon or late,
Grant me a welcome at Thy heavenly gate.

Easter Thoughts

As I advance through this vale of tears
And enter into my declining years,
I wonder when and where my road will end,
And I hope there to meet my one true Friend.

When I shall have passed through death's dark gates,
I know that judgment there for me awaits.
My hope is for a merciful assize
And that up to Heaven my soul will rise.

What good then Earth's goods and its many needs?
The only treasures of worth are good deeds
And any thoughts, words or actions of love –
These are what matter in Heaven above.

On this day of the Rising of the Lord,
He is my hope for eternal reward.

Glossary

A Tale

R&A	Royal and Ancient Golf Club of St Andrews
fey	supernaturally strange; portending death
drouthy	thirsty
maist	most
uncouthy	unfriendly; fear-inspiring

The Bonnie Links o' St Aundraes

whin	gorse
foozled	badly bungled

Whins, Will We See Your Like Again?

whin	gorse

To Another Mouse

wha	who
bickering brattle	rushing clatter
ken	know
maun	must
mair	more
sair	sore
blends	blinds
ee	eye

Bonnie Green Thing

tine	usually means 'to lose' but, in this context, means to aerate greens by making small holes in them

To A Mouse

sleekit	shiny coated
whyles	sometimes
ilka	each, every
ken	know
hale	whole
ca'	call
thy lane	alone
gang	go
aft	often
agley	awry
giest	givest

To A Computer

fa'	fall, befall
abune	above
wordy	worthy
licht	light
bricht	bright
eldritch	unearthly
nicht	night
onie	any
richt	right
weel-swall'd	well swelled
belyve	quickly

owre	over
haund	hand
wha's	who has
parritch	porridge
claes	clothes